THE ART of INVENTING

From Idea to Invention:
The Proven Path to Product Development

DAVID A. STREEN

The Art of Inventing

From Idea to Invention: The Proven Path to Product Development

David A. Streen

WeHelpAuthors.com

The Art of Inventing ™

ISBN #978-1-968841-14-0   Paperback
ISBN# 978-1-968841-15-7   Hardcover
ISBN# 978-1-968841-16-4   eBook
ISBN# 978-1-968841-17-1 AudioBook

Printed and published in the United States by:
We Help Authors Publishing House
For Bulk Order Discounts please visit: **WeHelpAuthors.com/bulk**

Dear valued reader,

I extend my heartfelt gratitude to you for reading this book on inventing and product development. Your decision means the world to me, and I am genuinely touched by your support. My sincere wish is that the content within these pages serves as a valuable resource in guiding you towards the successful and profitable realization of your ideas. Moreover, I hope you find joy in the journey, just as I have discovered a deep  passion for product development. May this book inspire and empower you throughout the exciting process ahead.

Warm regards,
Dave Streen

100% Original Content – No AI (Artificial Intelligence) was used in the creation or writing of this book or its images.

This book was written for my personal use. It helps me run my own company better and now I am proud to share it with you!

All PDF documents included in this book are available at:

InventingBook.com/forms

Note: *I advise downloading all of the forms before reading the book. Not only will this help make reading the smaller font easier, but it will encourage you to put them into practice right away.*

"A journey of a thousand miles begins with a single step" **and
you picking up this book was a huge first step!**

Dedicated to my loving wife, Stacy, who always supports me.
I always say behind every great man is a great woman....

rolling her eyes.

And to my beautiful and talented daughter Skyler:
The Skye's the Limit!

"God is the wind in my sails.
The wind cannot be seen directly
and neither can God
but just as you can see
the wind causing the ripples
on the water,
you can see God
in the achievements I've made."

— David A. Streen

Contents

Introduction

To paraphrase the words of one of my mentors, Keith Cunningham, in his book "The Road Less Stupid", it's not about having more brilliant ideas or making more money; rather, it's about making fewer mistakes, or as he puts it: "avoiding the dumb tax".

If I had the book you're holding in your hands back when I got started, I would have personally avoided making tens of thousands of dollars worth of mistakes and would have been able to earn ten times what I did each year. I would have faced fewer difficult decisions. I would have been out in front of things versus always putting out fires. I would have met more deadlines and overall would have operated much more smoothly and successfully. I am sharing this information with you so that your path will be much easier than mine was.

Understanding the fundamentals of product development will give you a greater appreciation of all of the products on the market and give you the understanding of why things are made the way they are.

I didn't go very deep into each topic in this book (it would be 10,000 pages long if I had), instead, I touch on the most important steps and give you just enough knowledge to get started without overwhelming you.

I share this blueprint with you in hopes of helping you reach your dreams and goals quicker and with more ease.

I am not writing this book as an expert but rather as someone in the trenches trying to figure things out myself, mostly learning as I go. To reach a high level of success I hit a lot of bumps in the road. I hope the lessons in this book will help smooth out your journey.

The first 5 years of inventing and developing products I was broke almost every step of the way, but I finally figured out better ways of doing things which helped me become extremely profitable and successful. I wrote this book to help share these better ways with you.

I have brought over 100 ideas to life (4 while writing this book!) and successfully continue to design and sell new products every day. I have also helped countless others start their companies and bring their ideas to market successfully.

It is my belief that most new inventors and entrepreneurs do not have the proper resources to help guide them.

Following the example of giants such as Steve Jobs (Apple), Bill Gates (Microsoft), Jeff Bezos (Amazon), and Elon Musk (Tesla) can help guide us and I do believe that all success leaves clues, however our own journey will be much different than theirs. We must concentrate on mastering the fundamentals and play the game at a level equivalent to our readiness.

This book will help you learn the lingo (product development language and terms) as well as provide an overview of the process in a simple and easy to understand format.

I love to see new products on shelves, especially from people I've inspired or helped, so please share your feedback and include me when you celebrate your wins!

Please use the following hashtags when sharing on social media to make sure I see it:

#inventing   #inventingbook   #davestreen

Part 1 - The BIG IDEA

"If at first the idea is not absurd, then there is no hope for it."

—Albert Einstein

Have an Idea

Chapter 1

First, I would like to point out that just about everyone we know has had "a million dollar idea" (or several) and all of them combined wouldn't buy you a cup coffee without doing the work and making things actually happen.

The blueprint you hold in your hands will help you recognize the things you need to do and how to tackle them yourself or find the right people to help you.

The first thing you need to be able to do is communicate your idea quickly and easily to anyone and everyone.

**WARNING: DO NOT COMMUNICATE YOUR IDEA
TO ANYONE UNTIL YOU READ CHAPTER 2**

Form Number 1 on the following page is designed to help you work through some of the basic elements and get you started on this long, but fun road of turning your thoughts into a real life product.

"If you can imagine it, you can create it." — William Arthur Ward

IDEA / CONCEPTION:

Caveman Drawings / Simple Sketches

Front View

Side View

Top View

Other

Problem it solves: _______________________________

Manufacturing process: _______________________________

Guestimate: $ _________ /unit

Will people just get it? ☐ Y ☐ N
(Understand without explanation) ⬇
How much explanation is needed? _______________________

Can it be manufactured? ☐ Y ☐ N
⬇
At what cost: $ _________ /per unit

Will it sell itself? ☐ Y ☐ N
⬇
If NO above, How much of an
uphill battle is it and is it worth it? _______________

Where will it be placed in the queue? _______________

What is it similar to? _______________________

What does it compete with? _______________________

How is it different? _______________________

EdgyTools.com

InventingBook.com/forms

To complete **Form Number 1,** draw some simple sketches reminiscent of what a caveman would carve into a cave wall, accompanied by a simple and straightforward description. Keep in mind that if a concept is overly complex or difficult to articulate, it might indicate a lack of complete understanding, be too ambitious for a first attempt, or present challenges that could impede your progress (and sales) or potentially discourage you altogether. Begin with something simple. Even with my years of experience in bringing over a hundred products to market, there are still projects which I am not yet ready to tackle.

Dan Sullivan (Founder of Strategic Coach®) says to always test your idea on **check writers** *(credit card swipers might be a more up-to-date term). This was another lesson I learned late. If you describe your idea to people, they will either say "that will never work" (more on this later) or they will tell you "it is a great idea and you are brilliant". Both statements are equally dangerous. The first might discourage you and crush your dreams but the second may make you overconfident which may lead to paying a dumb tax, investing time and money into something that won't sell.*

Testing on check writers (credit card swipers / buyers) essentially leads to getting a true answer. For instance, if you showed someone a product that peels carrots exceptionally well, someone might tell you that it is a great looking product that seems to be really useful and well designed. (You are on top of the world and nothing can stop you with this kind of positive feedback. You know that you have a home run peeler). However, if you go one step further and say, "Cool, I am so glad you like it! It can be yours right now for ten bucks." This is the moment when the true feedback starts. If they act so quickly that they break a fingernail reaching for their wallet, the confidence was well deserved and you might indeed have a winning carrot peeler. However, if they say "oh, no thanks, not right now. I am not ready to buy." then you may not have cause to be as enthusiastic.

*At the end of the day, if you believe in your idea, then go for it or maybe ask someone who has successfully done something similar for their opinion or help. Some good advice is to **only take advice from someone you would trade places with** or has successfully done what you are trying to accomplish.*

*The second product that I developed and brought to market was a flop. We spent way too much time getting it perfect before testing the market. This is where I learned the phrase **"analysis paralysis"**. In other words, I made about 50 working prototypes before trying to sell my first one. I should have tested the first few on check writers. This would have taught me that even had I perfected the design they still would not have purchased one.*

*Along the same lines of thinking as "test on check writers" is the **"give it away for free"** concept. This test is when you have some samples already made, take them to where your potential customers would be and try to give them one for free. If someone won't take it for free, then it's doubtful that you will be able to sell a bunch of them. Michael*

Miller taught me this concept. Michael is probably the most honest and trustworthy guy I have met in the product development space and I am grateful for his extensive help and advice.

Next, you will answer the question of **What Problem Does It Solve?** If it does not solve a problem or make someone's life easier or better, then why are you bringing it to market? Is it just for enjoyment or some other reason?

Then you will need to **make sure the product doesn't already exist or is not protected by someone else's patent.** This is known as Prior Art. You can start with some internet detective work on your own to see if you can find any products or images similar to your idea on your own. Even if your searches do not show anything similar, you may want a patent attorney to do a more thorough and extensive search.

It is well worth spending the money up front to save you from finding out the hard way after you have invested tons of time, money, and resources into an idea that you cannot pursue.

I know these answers may crush your dreams but it is better to know right out of the gate that a product can't go the distance than to find out months later and after great financial and time investments have already been spent. Don't fret, nobody is limited to just one great idea. You will have more and more amazing ideas, especially as you gain capabilities in this crazy world of bringing products to life.

Next, Ask yourself:

Can it be manufactured and if so, at what cost? You may not know this answer on your own or until you get further into the process. Keep this in mind and come back to it when you do know.

Will people just get it? When people see your new product, will they understand what it is and how it will help them? Will it need to be explained or will they need to be taught what it is and how to use it?

Will it sell itself? On first sight, will they rush to buy it or will they need a lot of exposure to your marketing in order to make the buying decision?

How much explanation will be needed? Will a quick statement or picture explain everything they need to know or will they need to try a sample or watch a video in order to understand the product?

Next Up: Protect the Idea

Protect the Idea
Chapter 2

Protecting your idea can be accomplished many ways, but most methods take a lot of time and money. So, before you begin, please ask (and think about) the following questions:

"Does my product need to be protected?"

and

"Should it be protected?"

Before we go further into these questions, I would like to point out that the crooks and evil players usually aren't who you might think they are. I learned this lesson through my ergonomic hand punch known as the Control Punch™ which is basically a modern ergonomic version of a nail set. I was worried that one of the big hardware chains would knock it off and steal the idea for themselves. I was told that I was worrying about the wrong people. My friend Michael said that the last thing a Big Brand Name Store wants is a David vs. Goliath style news article written about how they ripped off the little guy.

As it turns out this product was knocked off despite patent protection and other intellectual property (I.P.) being in place, but not by a big guy. It was brought to my attention that a small tool maker in Hungary had not only stolen my idea but they were actually using my photos and videos to promote their cheaply made copy cat version of my product.

When I called my patent attorney, she informed me that there was little I could do even though I had the law on my side.

This was because in order to go after them, I would have to pay her fees, as well as a translator, a Hungarian lawyer, and court costs. The starting estimate was going to cost me $50,000 minimum, which I absolutely could not afford at the time. Since I wasn't doing business in Hungary this did not really affect me anyway.

Instead, I chose to reach out to them professionally and tried to reason with them. This had little success.

Eventually, I called them out on their social media pages. This coupled with a negative review campaign made it so that the juice wasn't worth the squeeze for them. That actually worked.

Since then, this product's full blown non-provisional patent has been issued along with other protection so I am much more prepared to defend it.

With that little bit of knowledge from my story, let's dig into the question of **"Does my product need to be protected?"**. The answer to this question is typically pretty cut and dry and usually financially based.

Some things to consider are:

How large is the Industry?

Will the product be used by everyone in the industry?

What is the estimated demand?

How many units per year will be sold, for how many years, and at what profit?

Will the product be licensed or will I bring it to market myself?

If your new idea has the potential to change the world and be adopted by everyone, it's likely worth protecting, but if it is only going to be used by a tiny niche, you might want to skip the expense and hassle and go straight to market.

At the end of the day, you are reading this book and starting down this amazing yet challenging road either to make money, or to help people, or most likely some combination of both.

If you truly want to help people, then maybe instead of protecting the idea, you should share it or give it away to someone who can make it happen quicker and possibly even better. If you are doing it for the money (there's nothing wrong with that), then you want to be smart about it. Remember to avoid the dumb tax.

A story I found fascinating was that the modern three-point safety belt was perfected by Volvo engineer Nils Bohlin in 1959 – and its patent was given for free to the world. The invention has been credited with saving millions of lives worldwide. The reason that Volvo patented the invention was so that nobody else could. They spent a lot of resources protecting the idea and then gave it away because Volvo cares about people and they didn't want anyone's greed to prevent saving lives. Volvo did not want anyone else to patent the idea and then prevent others from including this amazing safety feature in their automobiles because of money.

You can start with an Internet search to find out which type of protection you will need and what the starting costs will be. The USPTO (United States Patent and Trademark Office) has a help center that you can call to get assistance with their website and forms but they will not offer legal advice.

You will want to **talk to an expert** about the different types of patents and the costs for filing them. Even though you can file patents yourself, my experience has proven to me that having a great patent attorney fill them out is worth every penny if you can afford it. No point in having a patent that is easy to work around or not be enforceable. I always strive for mine to be as bulletproof as possible.

Patents are very complex, but let's get started with the basics. There are **Design Patents** which are relatively inexpensive but can be easy to work around. If you hold a flashlight up to your product, the shadow cast on the wall is basically what you are protecting (the shape and appearance).

Utility Patents are much stronger but more expensive and tougher to get approved. These protect the utility or function of the product.

My Control Punch has a Utility Patent protecting anything struck by an object meant to deliver a force to another object while having a digit (finger or thumb) in it. With the Utility Patent, you make a bunch of claims and some get rejected so they will need to be removed or changed. My patent attorney tells me that if a patent gets approved on the first round, then she didn't do her job and the claims were not bold enough. I mention this so you are aware that the cost of filling out the application and the filing fees are just the tip of the iceberg. Each time something needs to be explained or argued it must be presented to the examiner, and the attorney punches back in on the time clock (often without prior approval - blank checks which you may want to put some restrictions on).

Utility Patents come in two flavors, **Provisional** and **Non-Provisional.** A provisional patent buys you some time to make your product and start selling it so you can test (or prove) the market demand. This allows you to use the money which the idea is generating to fund the more expensive non-provisional patent or find out that there is not sufficient market demand to justify going all-in on the idea. (If this is your first product, don't fool yourself, you probably won't be able to go fast enough to pull this off unless you have help. The non-provisional patent costs much more money but lasts longer (if approved) and has more legal power.

Whichever patent you apply for allows you to make the claim Patent Pending legally.

It is against the law to claim 'Patent Pending' if you have not officially filed your application.

Now to help you answer the second question, please consider the question of **"Should it be protected?"**. Think about whether or not you are in it for the money and if the money is going to be worth it. To clarify, if your idea solves the problem of feeding starving people and you want to bring it to the world, you might not want to protect it or others would be discouraged from implementing your idea. The other side of the coin is that sometimes it is better to spend the money on marketing and being the **FIRST TO MARKET** versus filing a patent. Patents can take years to get approved and that lost time may cost you big, especially on products with short life expectancies. The money spent on patents might be better spent buying a lot of ads and promotion which may yield you a bigger payday.

My rule of thumb is that I protect my big ideas and skip protecting the small ones. Also, if one patent can cover several products, I usually do it. I also have evolved to the point where I try to **only design products worth protecting**, the clear winners.

Again, this chapter was mainly to get you thinking and to familiarize yourself with some of the basic terms so the next time you discuss them, they aren't brand new to you. There are many other methods available to help you protect your idea as well, such as: Registered Trademarks, 3D Trademarks, Trade Dress, and others. We will not go into these now but I wanted to make you aware that there are many options.

Patents are complex and people devote their entire lives to studying and learning about them so my advice is to ask for referrals and hire an expert when you are ready.

Next Up: Beat Up The Idea

Beat Up the Idea
Chapter 3

(Keep repeating this Chapter until your product is ideal)

Developing your idea basically entails working through it. You want to THINK!

A side-note on thinking is that we all assume we do it but hardly any of us actually do. Please read The Road Less Stupid, which I mentioned in the intro. It is a brilliant book which really taught me a lot about what the author calls **"Thinking Time"**. *Note: I recommend getting the physical book and the audio book so you can get the most out of it.*

Get The Road Less Stupid and many other recommended books at:
WeHelpAuthors.com/books

While you are thinking through your idea, play the devil's advocate. Beat it up like it owes you money!

You will need to look at your idea like it is stupid, like it is junk, and find out everything that is wrong with it. Write it all down. **Then use the following questions as a checklist and solve the issues:**

How can it be better?

If cost wasn't a factor, what would make it even better?

What's the MVP? (Minimal Viable Product)

Minimal viable product is the bare bones, no frills cheapest way you can make it.

*Figure out what each end looks like and where you want (or need) to be on the **Money Line below:***

·—·

MVP   **High-End Version**

(Dirt Cheap)   (Price is no object)

(Draw a big X on the line above to mark the sweet spot)

So, for example, if I was designing a shovel, the **M**inimum **V**iable **P**roduct might be a common steel blade with an inexpensive wooden handle attached with a screw. The High-End Version might have a Titanium Blade with a serrated cutting edge, maybe an ergonomically shaped carbon fiber shaft, and a comfortable neoprene or leather wrapped handle. Maybe it will have a fulcrum to help leverage the lift. You get the idea. Just let your imagination run wild. I like to think: If someone like Elon Musk or Steve Jobs were designing it with their team and unlimited resources, what would they dream up? While you probably will not bring this version to market, it is a very important exercise. You might think of features that you can incorporate into your product that are affordable which you may not have thought of otherwise. This will also help you when filing certain patent applications.

After you have beaten your idea up, developed it further, and dialed in exactly what you think the perfect version to bring to market will be, I want you to go back to **Chapter 1** and do it all again with what you know now.

Fill out **Form Number 1** again using your newly gained knowledge and the details of the now more refined version of your product so you will be able to best communicate the idea to the right people such as the CAD Developers.

Non-disclosure Agreement (NDA) advised.

What the heck is a CAD Developer you might be asking? CAD stands for **c**omputer **a**ided **d**esign and is basically a manufacturing program that allows super smart guys to make pretty 3D drawings (known as renderings) of your product. This is when it starts to feel like your idea is coming to life. As with any service, I recommend getting referrals first but if you are new and don't even know who to ask for such a referral, then you can search online for some outsourcing platforms, or simply walk into a local machine shop and talk to someone. Odds are that if they make stuff, they can design the files too. If they do not do their own CAD work, they might be willing to recommend the person or company who does it for them to you.

I feel it is important at this time to point out that many people get confused and think their idea is their baby. IT IS NOT YOUR BABY! It is a product and it needs to be great but is not your baby. Sure you will pour your heart and soul into developing it and your blood, sweat, and tears will go into promoting it but remember through this process that products are made for buying and selling. Products are to be used to solve a problem or make something better. Your idea is not your baby, your legacy, or who you are as a person.

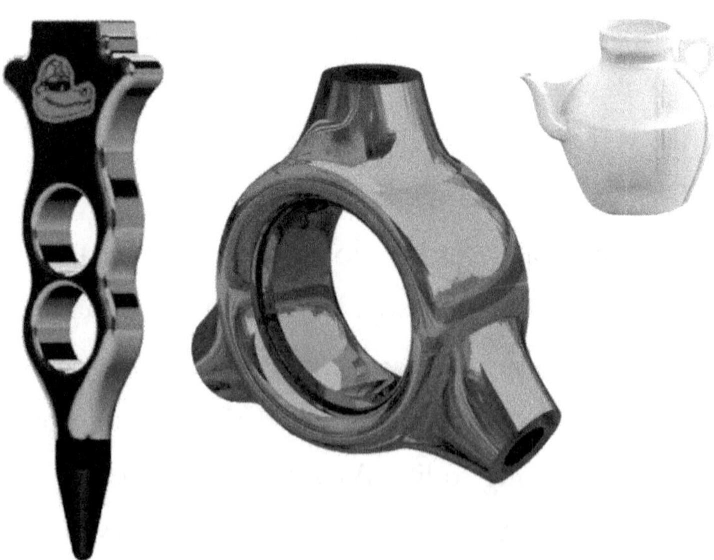

Here are a few examples of CAD Renderings

Do you have the CAD Drawings of your product now? Are you super excited? I bet you are! I know I am every single time I get a new one drawn! Please stop and celebrate this victory. I want you to realize you have just made it further than 99% of the people on the planet get with their ideas. **Enjoy and celebrate that accomplishment! I am proud of you!**

Seriously, please make sure you have paused and patted yourself on the back and enjoyed the great feeling because I am about to kick you in the proverbial nuts. I am sorry, but I need you to beat up your idea yet again. **This is critical to make sure you are bringing the best product to market and you will be able to get it manufactured at the best possible price.** Stop and THINK again. Go back and forth as often as needed.

If you have someone you trust with your life, you may want to trust them with your idea now and get their opinion. Don't ask Yes-Men who will tell you it's great, but at the same time avoid pessimists who will tell you it will never work. Look for someone knowledgeable who will give you solid feedback so you can make your product even better than it already is. Ideally, ask someone who would actually purchase and use your product. For example, I put a Control Punch™ in the hands of my handyman while he was working on my house.

As always, use your best judgment as well as legal advice, NDAS (Non-Disclosure Agreements), and anything else to protect you and your idea.

Once you are sure you have the design as good as it can be, get your CAD Files updated with any new changes or modifications and then get a 3D Sample Printed (if practical). This is the most affordable way I have found to get your idea in your hands so you can feel and test it.

Congrats! It's Celebration Time again! I am super proud of you! You have just taken a thought and made it solid! Your idea is actually in your hand! Celebrate that accomplishment!!

Now that you have a physical product in your hands, I need you to (you guessed it) beat it up yet again. Make changes. Do whatever needs to be done to get it dialed in to the exact product you want to see sold in stores. The product name WD-40 stands for **W**ater **D**isplacement – 40th attempt to perfect it. They probably could have turned out a decent product 39 times but wanted it to be the best. It has been selling well since 1953 so I think it was worth the extra effort they put into perfecting it.

The next step will be to find your manufacturer. You are ready to really play the game now! You will need to research and select the appropriate manufacturer. By appropriate, I mean find a company that has some experience and expertise making similar products or working with similar materials.

For example, if your idea is a balloon, you may want a rubber, latex, or mylar specialist. If your idea is a screwdriver, you may want a steel manufacturer. If your idea is a baby bottle, you may want a plastics specialist. This step might seem very difficult and maybe a bit overwhelming but it doesn't need to be. Most small scale manufacturing (which is where you are when you're starting) should be handled locally and a simple search on your phone or computer will show you where they operate. You may even drive past your ideal manufacturer or fabricator every day but have never paid attention to what they actually do in that building.

Dealing locally has so many benefits: you can meet face-to-face, you can communicate better, you can minimize or avoid expenses (like shipping, freight charges, and import duties), things tend to get handled quicker, and many other advantages too numerous to list.

The manufacturer you select should be knowledgeable about material selection which is important so that you get the best product for the best price which will perform as intended.

You may feel a little scared or intimidated to walk into one of these places for the first time but keep in mind that just like walking into a grocery store, you are the paying customer. They want your business and will be happy you are there. They will want to help you and do their best because they know that as you grow, they will get more business from you. The world of product development is a collaborative space where everyone works together in order to ensure everyone wins. As the saying goes: "Rising Tides Raise All Ships".

That being said, don't just rush in blindly. Although I believe that most people are good and will do the right things, some might wish to take advantage of a rookie. Don't let your lack of experience make you an easy target or a victim.

Note: I hesitated adding the prior warning because I do not want it to scare you into inaction. I want you to go for it, but proceed in a smart way with your eyes open.

Next Up: Test The Prototype

Test the Prototype
Chapter 4

Testing your idea in real life can be a roller coaster of emotions. If it works as expected (or even better than you could have hoped) then you are on top of the world, but if it fails, then that can be devastating. No matter what happens, it is not the end of the world. As my coach Dan Sullivan often reminds me "You are either on the winning team or the learning team". In other words, if your prototype is perfect, awesome! You get to pass go, collect $200, and move on to the next step. If your prototype is not ideal yet, you will have learned some valuable insights. The worst case scenario is that you learn that the product cannot be developed or cannot be developed for a price that makes sence.

Note: This may be why your idea doesn't already exist. Maybe others have had a similar idea but couldn't get over or around the hurdle you are facing. Please seek expert advice from several people before simply giving up and abandoning your idea. There may still be a solution that is not yet apparent.

It may also be a good idea to step back and focus on something else for a while. Coming back to a problem with a fresh perspective is often all that is needed to see new solutions.

Most likely you will be right in the middle of the two scenarios described. Your sample prototype is close but needs to be refined a little more. This is to be expected. Not even the best of the best knock it out of the park every time and especially not the first time at bat.

Form Number 2 (Page 28) is designed in a way that you will have a lot of valuable info regarding your product all in one place. The form is intended for you to fill out yourself and when the time comes, have a few inner circle people whom you trust completely also fill it out.

Note: You may or may not choose to have them sign a confidentiality agreement and/or an NDA (Non-Disclosure Agreement) or other legal documents to help protect your idea before showing it to them.

My company, EdgyTools®, uses humor in everything we do. Feel free to use the form as-is or recreate your own using the elements you like from mine. The important thing is to have a form and a process.

When **naming your product,** I like to advise my clients to keep it simple and easy to remember. Try to have the name say what the product does. For example, my Control Punch™ is a punch which offers superior control. My **Pull-Right Hook Tools™** are dent repair slide hammer hooks which allow more precision when pulling dents out of a vehicle. Since they are basically big hooks, we nicknamed them **"Hookers™"** and the body shop and Paintless Dent Repair guys get a huge kick out of it! I actually used to introduce myself by saying "Hi, I'm Dave Streen and I sell Hookers." It was a great ice-breaker that led to people asking for clarification or more info about what I do and it always got a laugh.

Our No-Roll Knockdown™ is a paintless dent repair (PDR) knockdown (*when a dent is pushed up too much during a repair, it needs to be knocked back down*) with a feature which prevents it from rolling away. You get the idea.

Basically, if you make a bar of soap that is easy to hold, call it the No-drop Soap, Drop No More Soap, or EZ Grip Soap. Don't call it the Wizamabang which says nothing about **what it is** or **what it does**. When marketing, **the easiest, clearest path always wins.** Don't confuse your potential customers. Don't make them have to work in order to figure out what your idea does and how it will benefit them. They won't. (More on marketing in Chapter 10)

When you first look at **Form #2** on the following page, you may notice a place for a Nickname for your tool or product. I have found that this may make it easier for your clients to remember and refer it to their friends and colleagues. As in my prior example, my clients always tease and laugh when they tell their buddies that they need to "Get Hookers from EdgyTools." It's just easier and more fun than saying Pull-Rite Hook Tools. So why not just use the fun nickname all the time? As you might imagine, some of my distributors may not wish to order Hookers; they want things to be more professional.

Please review the entire **Form #2** in order to familiarize yourself with it before moving on to the page after the form where I will explain each section in more detail.

So how do you refine your product? I use this form to help dial in the process:

Form #2

Tool Testing Summary

I promise that I will make make honest assessments:

Date Received: DateDue:

EdgyTools

Tool Tested:

Tool Name:

Funny Tool Nickname:

First Impressions - **Does the tool look cool, impressive, silly, etc.?**

(Write down your very first thoughts)

First Use: Describe the **One Major Thing** you notice the **first time.**

1

DESIGN (1 Worst - 10 Best)

Appearance 1 2 3 4 5 6 7 8 9 10

Function 1 2 3 4 5 6 7 8 9 10

Size 1 2 3 4 5 6 7 8 9 10

Effectiveness 1 2 3 4 5 6 7 8 9 10

Usefulness 1 2 3 4 5 6 7 8 9 10

Ease of Use 1 2 3 4 5 6 7 8 9 10

PRICE

The Price You Suggest

$__________.____

Highest Price You Would Pay:

$__________.____

No Brainer Price

$__________.____

Suggested Improvements
Example: Make it 1 inch longer

Best Feature About the Tool
Example: Built in O-Ring Groove

Benefits of the Tool the User experiences
Example: Better Control or Speed

Notes:
Example: This thing is badd-ass! Where has it been all my life
or What a hunk of crap. Is this a joke?

Would you bring this to market the way it is?
YES No

This is my honest evaluation: **X**__________________

InventingBook.com/forms

<u>FILLING OUT FORM NUMBER 2:</u>

FIRST IMPRESSIONS:

Do you love how your product looks? Does it look cheap or well made? Does it intrigue you? Will people know right away what it is and what it does or is it going to need a lot of explaining? Do people just get the concept?

Write these thoughts down on the form.

ONE MAJOR THING:

The very first time you looked at your new sample, what did you notice? What immediately caught your eye? Quick, write down your thoughts as you will soon move on and forget this important info. What you noticed first may be what your potential buyers will also notice first. If it is a good thing, great! If it is a negative thing, how can you change or improve the issue?

The first time you held your idea in your hands, what did you feel? Was it heavier or lighter than you expected? Was it slippery or grippy? Did it feel like a quality product? Was it comfortable to hold and use? Again, write these things down as you are experiencing them. Like the old saying goes, you don't get a second chance at a first impression.

Write these thoughts down on the form.

ACTUAL PRODUCT DESIGN:

Appearance: Does it look the way you thought it would or should? If you could describe your idea with one word, what would it be?

Cool? Elite? Novel? Silly? Fun? Professional? High-end?

Think of your one word and then evaluate how well your sample product captures the essence of your one word.

Circle Your Answer

Function: Does it work? Does it accomplish what it is meant to do? Does it do it well? Could it be improved?

Circle Your Answer and Make Notes Below

Size: Did it turn out to be the size you envisioned? Would it be better if it was a little smaller or larger? Should part of it be narrower or wider? How could the size and shape be improved? Put some serious thought and consideration into this question.

Circle Your Answer and Make Notes Below

Effectiveness: Is your prototype effective? Does it do what it is intended to do? Does it do it the best it can or could a little change make it more effective? Does it work like a dream?

Circle Your Answer and Make Notes Below

Usefulness: Is it as handy as you thought it would be? If yes, great. If no, can the idea be refined or adapted in order to better solve the problem your idea is designed to help with? Does it need an accompanying product or part to help it work better? What else could be changed, added, or subtracted to make it even more useful?

Circle Your Answer and Make Notes Below

Ease of Use: Is the product easy to use right from the start or is there a learning curve needed to get accustomed to using it? Is it awkward or is it easy and comfortable to hold?

Circle Your Answer

PRICE:

Prices can be determined in many ways. I will go into some of the most common methods now.

The Price You Suggest is basically the first number that pops into your head that you would expect the product to cost. Believe it or not, the number you pull out of thin air is actually based on thousands of product pricing experiences and knowledge accumulated over your lifetime and it happens almost instantly in your subconscious. Trust the number that comes from your gut!

Write this number down.

The Highest Price you would pay is the absolute top dollar you could ever see yourself paying. If you really, really wanted it and the timing was perfect, what would you spend? This is similar to charging **whatever the market will bear.** Said another way is the humorous line that goes "Charge 'em 'til they holler and then back down a dollar." In other words, the highest price someone else would possibly pay. Note: This is a little different from the highest price you would pay because you are not your customer. You will have different biases than they do.

Write this number down.

Some of the perks of this pricing method are that high prices are often associated with high quality. You might actually sell more of your product because it is priced higher. I know this sounds counter-intuitive but if you think about your own purchases, you will remember times this has worked on you. I am sure that you have experiences where you were correct and it was very wise to go with the highest priced item as it truly was the best. I am also sure that you have had the opposite experience where the highest priced item was a let down. Just keep this in mind as you start to figure out your own pricing strategy.

The No-Brainer Price is a price that is so low, you would buy extras to give away or have as backups. This is the irresistible price. An example of an irresistible price is when you come home from the store with a new product you didn't even really want but your brain wouldn't let you pass up that good of a deal. (Admit it, you've done this, we all have.)

Now that you have these three prices written down, let's dig a little deeper into what they really mean and why we are figuring them out right now.

Another way to calculate your ideal price is to use the **comparison pricing method.** Look at similar items and see how they are priced. You can take an average, land anywhere near the middle or closer to either end. You can always lower your price, or have a sale, but it's tough to raise your price.

A common mistake it to compete on price. Trying to be the lowest price is a losing strategy based on lack of knowledge or low confidence levels, yet this is precisely what most people do. You often do not know all of the true expenses associated with marketing and fulfilling your product so you end up with less profit or even selling at a loss. You want/need to be profitable, not just a revolving door of money.

Some more things to consider:

If you are going to sell direct through someone else's platform, the fees may be reasonable and you will get to hold onto a big chunk of the revenue. These platforms can get you in front of a lot of eyes (potential customers) and offer many other advantages but they can also cut into your profits by charging fees and percentages.

If you are going to package the product yourself and sell it on your own website, there will be more costs involved such as website design and development, hosting your website, advertising and marketing, shipping, and many additional expenses that you will need to consider (including your time).

If you are going to **license your product**, then your role gets much easier and the risk is greatly reduced but the profit margin gets much thinner. I remember being shocked and insulted the first time I heard that I would only make between 2-6% of the gross depending on my patent status. At the time, I thought this was absurd. Now (in hindsight and with more knowledge) I know it was truly generous and fair. Think about it this way, would you rather have 100% of ten thousand or 4% of ten million. I'll take the 4% all day long and I bet you are thinking that sounds pretty great too. Don't get caught up on percentages especially while you are learning.

The next section of the form is to help you figure out what is great about your idea. **Answering these simple questions now and adding to them as your product continues to evolve and develop** will help you when it comes time to market and promote your finished product.

The "**Notes:**" section of the form is for you to write down any and all thoughts. Just get them out of your head and written down. It may not be obvious now how this will help you but trust me, it will help keep your head clear and I promise these notes will come in handy each time you review this form.

The Final Question to ask is: **"WOULD YOU BRING THIS PRODUCT TO MARKET THE WAY IT IS?"** This will help give you real clarity. Is it ready? Is there absolutely nothing else needing to be improved or changed? If the answer is yes, then pop the cork and pour some champagne! It's celebration time again!

Note: *You can use sparkling apple cider or grape juice (or any special treat) to celebrate if you do not partake in alcohol consumption. The idea is to celebrate your victories and acknowledge your accomplishments!*

<u>Bonus:</u> Put yourself in other people's shoes and re-ask the question. If you are a fan of the popular show Shark Tank, pretend you are each one of the sharks. Would Mark Cuban bring this product to market the way it is or if not, what would he suggest changing? How about Mr. Wonderful or Daymond John or Lori Greiner? If you have not seen the show, I would suggest binge watching it as you will get valuable insights into the product development world. I would also like to point out that there are real life sharks who are not sharks at all who will help you. To clarify, I am talking about people who help put new products on shelves and land deals who are not cut throat or doing things a certain way because they need ratings. I am not bagging on the sharks on Shark Tank at all, they are amazing business people and have made a lot of people's dreams come true. I am simply pointing out that people are not all money driven and there are extremely knowledgeable people who love finding new products and helping new product developers like us. They have helped me and I know they will help you too when you (and your idea) are ready.

Dave Streen (Author / Inventor / Product Developer)

and

Daymond John (Shark Tank and FUBU)

Genius Network® Annual Event 2023

Daymond shared an impactful story. He told us how his mom said to him that everything we see in the world all started with one person who had one idea who took one action. She told him that it could be him that did things like this. **It all started with one person.** *It was somebody who just took the blindfold off and just said they could do it.*

I hope this book encourages you to realize the same!

PART 2 - Making the Thing

The Model T Ford

"Any customer can have a car painted any colour that he wants... so long as it is black."

—Henry Ford

The Manufacturing Package
Chapter 5

A manufacturing package is basically a fancy name for all of the files, artwork, and supporting documents which a manufacturer will need to make your product. These files must be prepared well. After all, you aren't buying a box of cookies from your niece. You are buying product made in large quantities (bulk) and both you and your manufacturer need to be on the exact same page with all of the variables.

How many units will be made?

When and how will they be picked up or delivered?

What materials will be used?

What finishes will be used?

Will the product have "Retail Ready" packaging done by the manufacturer or will you do it or have it done after you have received the product and inspected the quality?

These are just a few of the many, many things which need to be decided before both parties can agree to move forward.

These variables are all addressed on forms known as **P**ro-forma **I**nvoices and **P**urchase **O**rders (PI and PO for short. Also abbreviated as P.I. and P.O.) and they are so important that I have devoted a chapter for each of them. For now, just know that a P.I. (Pro-forma Invoice) is sent to you from the manufacturer (you need to request the P.I. and send the manufacturing package along with the request for them to work from). The manufacturer will essentially provide a detailed quotation specifying the number of units they will produce for you and at what cost, taking into consideration all the variables we will discuss. The Purchase Order (P.O.) will be highly redundant, essentially a duplicate copy the Proforma Invoice (P.I.). However, the P.O. serves as your official contract offer to the manufacturer, indicating your agreement to the terms they've outlined and giving them the official go-ahead to commence production. We will delve deeper into these details in following chapters.

Now back to the **manufacturing package**. Some of the items that may be included will be the finalized CAD drawings, line art for any etchings (See examples on page 41), material and finish details, dimensions, acceptable tolerances, manufacturing details, and anything else which helps clarify what the finished product will be. Please don't get overwhelmed or confused by this manufacturing package. Your CAD developer will likely provide you with all of the files you will need and you can simply forward the email attachments to the manufacturer.

Line Art Example
Line art is a scalable drawing which may represent etching or other manufacturing details

The manufacturer has your back as they do not want costly mistakes or delays either. They are usually experts at this process since this is what they do for a living. They will typically be very experienced and will be able to spot lacking or incorrect information as well as any other possible issues. They will not only point them out to you, but will more than likely offer guidance and solutions.

When you send the manufacturing package over and request a P.I. (Pro-forma Invoice – Your estimate or quote for manufacturing) you may want to ask for various quantities. Try to match your desired quantities with the proper size manufacturer. Do not expect a manufacturer that makes 1 million pieces a month for their clients to bend over backwards for your order of 100 units. You will want to request two or three quantities to see if you can take advantage of **economies of scale discounts**. To put it simpler, sometimes ordering more units will greatly reduce the per unit price and other times it will not.

There is an old joke which is almost always true that goes "There is Speed, Quality, and Price but you can only pick 2".

For my paintless dent repair tool company, EdgyTools®, LLC, I typically will request a P.I. for the following quantities: 1,000 units, 2,500 units, and 5,000 units. This will give enough incentive for the manufacturer to pass along any savings which may be available. There are a lot of factors on their end which they are considering. How busy they are (do they want the extra work), machine set-up times, and cleanup may be some of the more obvious ones. Maybe the raw material MOQ (Minimum Order Quantity - smallest amount they will sell) will dictate how many units of your product will be ideal to produce.

When I receive a P.I. from a manufacturer I can usually do some quick math and know how many units I will order.

Example 1:

If I get back numbers like:

1,000 Units = $1.00

2,500 Units = $0.50

5,000 Units = $0.22

In this example, you can clearly see that I will be stretching to order as many as I possibly can in order to maximize my profit. In fact, with numbers reducing in this drastic way, I would probably request a new PI asking for even higher quantities like 10,000 and 25,000 units.

Example 2:

If I get back numbers like:

1,000 Units = $1.00

2,500 Units = $0.99

5,000 Units = $0.97

In this example, you can see that there are hardly any savings being realized. Therefore, it is probably in my best interest to minimize my risk and investment by simply starting with the quantity of 1,000 units.

Please keep in mind that these quantities and prices are fictitious. (I made the numbers up in order to illustrate the concepts.) Your quantities may range anywhere from only ordering only 1 or 2 units to 1,000,000 units or more. Whatever quantities you are needing, it is always best to know if quantity based price reductions are going to be substantial. It is also recommended to request a P.I. from more than one manufacturer.

IMPORTANT NOTE: *Anytime you share your idea, you may be risking someone stealing it. As always, I advise you to seek legal council and use your best judgment when it comes to trusting anyone. NDAs and Non-Competes are usually a good idea.*

One comment which I feel is worth noting is that the P.I. is not an obligation, commitment, or binding contract so you may request them without fear. Even if you do not think you will make a purchase but want to see what numbers come back. The other side of that coin is **please be respectful and considerate of the manufacturer's time and effort.** The manufacturer needs to do a lot of homework that may involve many people, phone calls, emails, etc. to prepare an accurate P.I. Statement so please do not request ones that you know you will not be acting on. You don't want to be the little boy who cried wolf too many times or when you really need a P.I. from a manufacturer, they may not want to waste their time again. You can always be up-front and let them know that you will probably not be placing an order but would like to know a ballpark price that you could expect to see if the project was to move forward.

Next Up: Get a Quote

Get a Quote (Request a P.I.)
Chapter 6

Pro-forma Invoices were introduced to you in the previous chapter but let's dig a little deeper into what this actually might look like and some of the info you can expect to see on one.

Please remember from Chapter 5, that you will not receive a Pro-forma Invoice without **first requesting one** and **supplying the basic details** such as what you want manufactured and the quantity. You will need to note things such as the materials used, style of finish(es) selected, any etching or markings, as well as the address which the order will be shipped to, and the date of the expected delivery. Other variables you will want to lock down might be how the product is packaged and how it is to be shipped or picked up.

The manufacturer(s) will usually do the heavy lifting and supply you with most of this info and may simply ask questions to verify or fill in any missing details they need so you do not need to feel overwhelmed. Requesting a P.I. is pretty simple and painless. Reviewing the P.I. is when you really want to **focus and concentrate**.

Again, I recommend requesting P.I.s from more than one manufacturer to make sure you are getting realistic and fair rates. Select 2 or 3 manufacturers and request 3 Quantities from each. Specify the materials and other details. Pay attention to more than just the numbers. Were they quick to reply? How was the communication? Did any red flags pop up? Etc.

Reviewing a PI: I suggest you print out the P.I.(s) (assuming it is emailed to you) and taking it to a quiet place to avoid interruptions and distractions. I like to sit by a lake or somewhere in nature. Wherever you decide to do this, this is when you really want to have your thinking cap on so that you can avoid any costly or timely mistakes or delays. (Remember to **avoid the Dumb Tax**) Trust me, I have paid the dumb tax (made costly mistakes) many times including but not limited to accidentally ordering parts made from the wrong material, having parts etched incorrectly, ordering incorrect quantities, you name it. Most of my costly mistakes were made from going too fast (usually to meet some trade-show or other fictitious deadline). Many of these mistakes could have easily been avoided had proper thinking time been taken.

Remember: Slow is smooth and smooth is fast!

You may wish to print and fill out **Form Number 3: Break Even Analysis Sheet** (please modify my example to fit your needs) to help make sure you are being honest with yourself on whether or not it is a **wise investment** to order the product. I know this may be soul crushing after coming this far with your idea but trust me, it is better to pull the plug at this point than to tie up money with product inventory which may not move fast enough.

I recommend that you make your own Break Even Analysis Sheet using your numbers and variable expenses which may be very different from mine.

Add notes or triggers to help you avoid paying any dumb taxes.

Form Number 3: Break Even Analysis Sheet

R&D

    Consulting
    CAD Work $

Samples $

Testing $

Production Run $

Packaging Supplies & Labor $

WebPage & Ad Design & Mail Chimp, etc $

Total Production Costs: $ ______________

Production Run Quantity: ______________

TPC / QTY = $__________ (Production Cost per Unit)

Times Multiplier (Typically 4-5) = **$_______ (Sug. Retail Price)**

Times Wholesale Discount: (.65) = **$_______ (Wholesale Price)**

Wholesale Less TPC = $________ (Profit per Unit)

TPC / Wholesale Price = # Pre-orders for Break even _____________

* Factor in for Marketing, Shipping, Giveaways & Donations

Ask wholesalers for Preorder commitments or checks.

InventingBook.com/forms

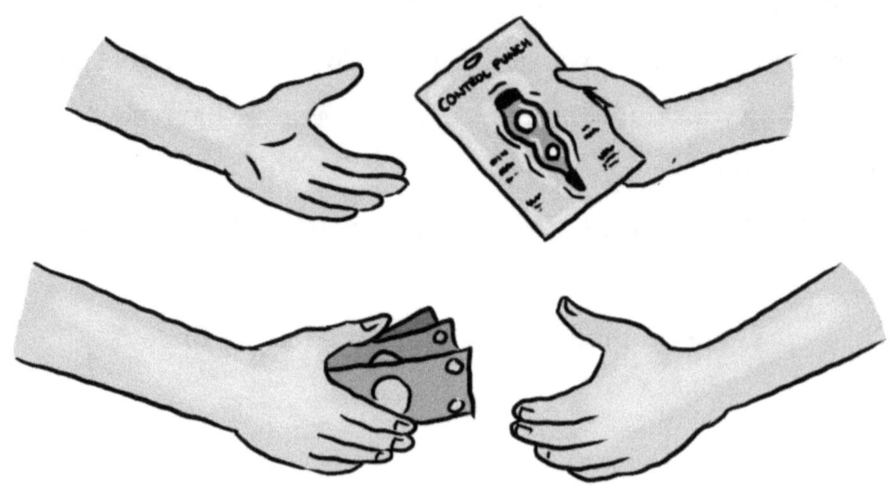

Next Up: Buy It

Buy It (Issue a P.O.)
Chapter 7

Purchase Orders are basically short little contracts between you (the buyer) and the Manufacturer (the seller).

Hint: The term buyer and seller can be easy to confuse as you will play both roles with your product. Put as simply as possible, right now you are buying the product, which you intend to sell to others, so you are the buyer first. Once you have your product manufactured, you will switch hats and become the seller.

A **Purchase Order** (P.O.) is pretty much copying and pasting the info from the P.I. into another form but it's still important to be careful with this step. You really want to **stop and think** as you create your P.O., especially when you are new to the process.

There are many ways to issue a P.O. including software designed specifically for this, pre-made forms, and many other options. I prefer to use the one I made myself. (See **Form Number 4** on page 53)

Please keep in mind that my company is a little silly and fun so you will probably choose to use a more professional version. I created mine to help me avoid making simple mistakes. I included sections to help remind me of details which can be easily overlooked. I recommend doing the same, or at minimum, **create a checklist which you use each time you create a Purchase Order** (P.O.).

The process of creating a P.O. is not overly complicated but it does need to be done with extreme accuracy. A little preparation will help you succeed. While some aspects like material selection or etchings are entirely your decision, while others are negotiable. Certain details such as production or delivery speed may be dictated by the manufacturer. Quantity may also influence the terms.

For example, if you are ordering a very small quantity, the manufacturer may require the full payment up front before they start. This may be because they need to order the raw materials and the total amount of money involved for the project is not enough to make splitting the payment and handling receivables worth it to them. The flip-side of this situation would be the manufacturer not requiring any payment up front but I would not expect this until you have a relationship and trust built up over years, if ever. Typically, terms such as these will be negotiated.

Some payment terms which are common would be 30% deposit with the remainder due when manufacturing is complete but before releasing the goods (shipping your product). 50% down with 50% upon completion is also very common or it may be 70% down with 30% upon completion. Anything is possible but please remember, **anything can be negotiated** so don't hesitate to ask.

This is probably a new relationship and you don't want to get burned but neither does the manufacturer. They are the ones with a track record and history of performance so you must look at things from their perspective as well as your own.

How the payment is sent may also be an important term to clarify. For example, can you use a credit card to take advantage of points or rewards as well as being able to make payments if needed? For global orders, you can use an electronic payment or a money app for sending small money amounts (under $500 - usually for samples), and I recommend that you send a Wire Transfer for any amount over $500. Use whatever methods you deem safe and feel comfortable using.

Some items to have on your P.O. might include:

Material(s)

Coatings

Finish

Etchings *(Artwork or details supplied by you)*

SKU# *(See Chapter 8)*

UPC# *(Also in Chapter 8)*

Patent Pending or **Patent#**

Retail Ready Packaging Instructions and Artwork *(This is the packaging for how your product will look on the shelf of a store - How each individual product is packaged)*

Packaging for Delivery *(This is how all of the bulk Retail Ready Pieces will be packaged - pieces per carton, cartons per pallet, etc. as well as how the items will be protected for transit.)*

Partial Delivery Levels / Conditions

Shipping Methods and Rates

Duties and Fees: Codes and Rates *(If applicable)*

Images

Manufacturing Package *(Double checked for accuracy and reviewed with CAD Developer)*

Benchmarks / Supporting Products / Materials *(You may choose to send the best samples back to the manufacturer along with complete instructions to help ensure all of the details and standards are well established and adhered to. These are called benchmark samples.)*

Any videos, photos, or anything else you can think of to help ensure you get exactly what you envision, want, and expect.

NOTE: *I almost always request a PI for Production Ready Samples to be approved by me prior to the start of production. This allows me to pay for the final samples and the production run all at once (saves time and fees) but actually get the first items off the press in my hands to evaluate. This usually costs a few hundred dollars extra (depending on the product) but has saved my butt many times. The exception of this would be if I'm reordering a product with no changes (which has been made by the same manufacturer before); in this situation a video from the manufacturer showing the first run production parts will often suffice.*

Form Number 4: Blank Purchase Order

QTY: _______________

Unit Price: _____________ USD

Express Shipping: _______ USD

Total Price: $_________.___ USD

30% Down: $_________.___ USD

70% Due: $_________.___ USD

Purchase Order #:___________

Date: ____/____/________

Ship To:

SKU#: _______________

Product Name: ________________

Manufacturing Number: __________

Material: ________________

Hardening: ________________

Prepping: ________________

Finish: ________________

NOTES: ________________

Etching Images / Details:

Assembly:

Retail Packaging Details and File Links:

Shipment Packing Instructions:

Delivery on or before: ____/____/________
Note: Delays more than 30 days may be subject to 5% monthly reduction if not communicated clearly

Payment Terms and Performance Conditions:

1) Payment terms:
30% deposit upon acceptance of P.O. by Supplier, with balance of payment contingent on Performance Conditions noted below, prior to product shipment.

2) Performance Conditions:
Compliance with Description and Manufacturing drawings/data is necessary during the entire manufacturing process. At completion of mass production, an accurate **Outgoing Inspection Report** *is to be provided, along with visual evidence of order compliance* **(Photos and/or Video)**. *Upon acceptance of the OIR and visual presentation, the balance of payment will be promptly remitted along with written authorization for the release of product shipment.*

Important Precautions:

Example: If threaded rod is used, pay close attention to thread depth. If thread lock is used, please make sure it is fresh and proper drying time is allowed.

Manufacturer:

Seller Approval: X________________
Please sign and Return

Buyer Approval:
X________________

THANK YOU!!

InventingBook.com/forms

Next Up: SKU#s, Barcodes, UPC, Etc.

SKU#s, Barcodes, UPC, Etc.
Chapter 8

Looking back, it should have been common sense for me to implement SKU#s right away. I mean any kid could tell you that when you make your second product you should call them Thing One and Thing Two or some easy system for keeping track of them, especially if you use silly names like I do. Unfortunately, this didn't occur to me until year 4 of running my business when I had already brought over 50 products to market.

When I did finally wake up and realize that I needed a better system, **I put some thought into my product line as far as where it currently was as well as where it was headed.**

I decided to use *ET-* as the prefix for the SKU numbers (standing for EdgyTools-) of the products I created. I created similar prefixes for other manufacturers whose products I also carried at the time. Then I used a number system which made sense and would grow as my product line grew.

I used the following system:

001-099 - Knockdown Tips

100-199 - Pushing Tips

200-299 - Low Profile Tips

300-399 - Caps

400-499 - Knockdown Tools

500-599 - Hangers / Leveraging Devices

600-699 - Accessories

700-799 – Tapes

800-899 - Bundles

900+ - Replacement Parts and Misc.

For example, when I developed a new soft cap *(Used to cover my dent repair tips to protect the e-coating on the back side of the vehicle panel)*, I would simply assign the next available number in the 300 block of numbers. (Example ET-306)

I placed these SKU numbers on the product packaging, the product pages on the website, and even assigned 301 Redirects using them. If you aren't web savvy, this simply means that if you typed EdgyTools.com/1 into the search bar of your internet browser, you would go right to the product which is assigned ET-001, Same goes for an ET-418, simply type EdgyTools.com/418 and you will be automatically directed to the No-Roll Knockdown (ET-418) page. Along the same lines, I use 301 redirects in other ways, for example, at the time of this writing, if you go to WedgeLight.com, you will automatically be redirected to the Wedge Light™ page on EdgyTools® website and you will notice this SKU# is a WL-1 because I have partners on this product. When we create our second Wedge Light, can you guess the SKU#? That's right, it will be a WL-2 unless we wish to skip a block of numbers and make it a WL-10.

There is no right or wrong way to assign SKU numbers and they can be as long or short as you like. The idea is to use them to make your life and everything you do easier.

For example, tracking inventory is much easier for me now. So is filling orders. If I asked you to grab me a Medium Control Punch made of Stainless Steel out of my garage you'd be like "huh?". But if I asked you to grab me an ET-406, you would just start looking at the numbers on the packaging and grab the one clearly labeled ET-406 (right between the ET-405 and the ET-407 - See how easy it is now?) and you would have grabbed the correct item without needing to know anything about the product or its name.

Along the lines of making things easier, UPC Barcodes and QR codes can be created to help you sell on larger platforms. These also allow you (and your resellers) to scan an item just like at the grocery store. This is a bit more complex to set up properly and you are probably not to the stage where it matters yet anyway.

On the following page, you will find an example of the form I use to track my inventory as it goes from my house, to storage, to packaging, to the fulfillment center, or anywhere else my products may travel. I recommend you make a similar form to start using even if this is your only product as it will start good habits and allow you to know what you have on hand and where it is located. A lot of software and platforms assist you with transfers but I have found that good old pen and paper is the most reliable as well as being easy and efficient. I keep a stack of them printed out ahead of time so they are ready to go as soon as I need one. Please go with whatever method you prefer as long as it is accurate and helps you manage your inventory and transfers well.

EdgyTools.com — Product Inventory Transfer Worksheet   Date: ______________

From:	To:

NAME	SKU#	TYPE	QTY
Gator Tooth (BM)	ET-001	RR / BULK	
Gator Tooth (Tiki)	ET-002	RR / BULK	
Rocket Ship	ET-003	RR / BULK	
Pirate Peg Leg (Tiki)	ET-004	RR / BULK	
Mirror Polished (SS)	ET-005-SS	RR / BULK	
Mirror Polished (Tit)	ET-005-Tit	RR / BULK	
B-Cup Knockers	ET-006	RR / BULK	
Crown Killer 2.0	ET-007	RR / BULK	
C-Cup Knockers (Dipped)	ET-008	RR / BULK	
D-Cup Knockers	ET-009	RR / BULK	
Ooh La La (Tiki)	ET-13	RR / BULK	
Flat Tip (Pushing)	ET-101	RR / BULK	
Golf Tee	ET-102	RR / BULK	
Big Bullseye (Formerly V-Tip)	ET-103	RR / BULK	
Tank Tip (Formerly Stubby)	ET-104	RR / BULK	
HEF-T (Golf Tee 2.0)	ET-105	RR / BULK	
3-in-1 Tip	ET-106	RR / BULK	
Thumper Hybrid	ET-108	RR / BULK	
Little Pecker	ET-201	RR / BULK	
Tiny Crown Killer	ET-202	RR / BULK	
Tiny Bullseye	ET-203	RR / BULK	
The Crease Release	ET-204	RR / BULK	
Polished KNOB (Knockdown)	ET-205	RR / BULK	
KNOB Pushing Tip (SS)	ET-206	RR / BULK	
A-Cup Knockers	ET-207	RR / BULK	
Tiny Variety Caps	ET-300	RR / BULK	
Crown Killer Variety Caps	ET-301	RR / BULK	
Thumper Variety Caps	ET-302	RR / BULK	
B-Cup Pasties Variety Caps	ET-303	RR / BULK	
Little Pecker Anvil Rocket Ship (BM)	ET-312	RR / BULK	

NAME	SKU#	TYPE	QTY
C.P. Aluminum Small	ET-401	RR / BULK	
C.P. Aluminum Medium	ET-402	RR / BULK	
C.P. Alum Large	ET-403	RR / BULK	
C.P. SS Small	ET-405	RR / BULK	
C.P. SS Medium	ET-406	RR / BULK	
C.P. SS Large	ET-407	RR / BULK	
C.P. Tit Small	ET-409	RR / BULK	
C.P. Tit Medium	ET-410	RR / BULK	
C.P. Tit Large	ET-411	RR / BULK	
The Finger "Ding Ring"	ET-417	RR / BULK	
No-Roll™ Knockdown	ET-418	RR / BULK	
C.P. HW Alum Small	ET-419	RR / BULK	
C.P. HW SS Small	ET-420	RR / BULK	
Regular Hanger (Black)	ET-501	RR / BULK	
DentCraft Black Hanger Orig.	ET-501-DC	RR / BULK	
Magnum (XL) Hanger (Red)	ET-502	RR / BULK	
Ninja Flat Bar Hanger (Green)	ET-503	RR / BULK	
3 - Way Step Hanger (Purple)	ET-504	RR / BULK	
The Strap On Hail Hanger	ET-505	RR / BULK	
Pull-Rite Hook Tools "Hookers"	ET-601	RR / BULK	
Damage Evaluator	ET-602	RR / BULK	
The Hack Pack	ET-603	RR / BULK	
Tire Tower	ET-616	RR / BULK	
Restore Block - Fine	ET-625	RR / BULK	
Restore Block - Medium	ET-626	RR / BULK	
Restore Block - Rough	ET-627	RR / BULK	
Gator Glide	ET-628	RR / BULK	
PDR Tool Restoration Kit	ET-629	RR / BULK	
3/4" Alum Extension	ET-640	RR / BULK	
1" Alum Extension	ET-641	RR / BULK	

NAME	SKU#	TYPE	QTY
EdgyTape	ET-701	RR / BULK	
Tear-able Tape	ET-702	RR / BULK	
Smallest EdgyTabs (6 Pack) - 11 mm	ET-703	RR / BULK	
Dime Tabs (6 Pack) - 16 mm	ET-704	RR / BULK	
Nickel Tabs (6 Pack) - 21 mm	ET-705	RR / BULK	
Half Dollar Tabs (6 Pack) - 28 mm	ET-706	RR / BULK	
Variety Pack (8 Pack) - 2 of Each	ET-707	RR / BULK	
Huge Variety Pack (24 Pack) - 6 of Each	ET-708	RR / BULK	
Release Agent Bottle & Sprayer	ET-709	RR / BULK	
Knockdown Bundle	ET-801	RR / BULK	
Pushing Tip Bundle	ET-802	RR / BULK	
Huge Tiny Weenie Bundle	ET-803	RR / BULK	
Hail Rod Tip Bundle	ET-804	RR / BULK	
Knockers Bundle	ET-805	RR / BULK	
Gator Snap Bundle	ET-806	RR / BULK	
How's it Hanging Bundle	ET-807	RR / BULK	
Hookers and Hangers Bundle	ET-808	RR / BULK	
Cap Guide Everything Bundle	ET-810	RR / BULK	
Slip-Not Tip Grip	ET-900	RR / BULK	
C.P. Steel Strike Plate Refill	ET-901	RR / BULK	
No-Roll Grip Refill	ET-902	RR / BULK	
Edgy Partner Starter Kit	ET-950	RR / BULK	
Banner	ET-999	RR / BULK	

☐ **Shopify Levels Adjusted**

InventingBook.com/forms

Next Up: Packaging

Packaging
Chapter 9

Packaging helps sell products! Did you know that many super successful companies sometimes spend more on the packaging than they do on the actual product? This baffled me the first time I heard it. I was told Disney collectible pins are an example of this, but I have not confirmed it. **Packaging can be the difference between a customer buying the product or not.** That's how important packaging can be. You may want to consider hiring a professional packaging designer.

When I first started developing products, I would hand wrap them in tissue paper with the help of my wife and daughter. We wrapped our dent repair tools like a luxury store would wrap fine crystal. LOL

Roll forward to our second year and we found some really nice zip bags similar to what you might buy quality trail mix in. We added stickers printed on our home computer and eventually added nice folded toppers which we hole punched so our products could hang on pegboard hooks. We were so proud and thought our products looked like a million bucks. Nobody in our tiny industry had ever really paid much attention to retail packaging before. We were among the first. Now many of them use retail ready packaging for their products as well.

After being in the game for almost a decade, I am learning more and more about **Retail Ready Professional Packaging**. As with anything, there are pros and cons to having products professionally packaged for you. Some of our products now come ready to sell and they look professional enough that we could sell them in big box stores. The downside is that we no longer get to personally inspect every single unit with the **Quality Control (QC) checklist** so there is a slight possibility that something with a defect may slip past us.

We have implemented stricter QC standards at the manufacturing level and again before packaging by a third party inspection service. Once the product arrives, we use spot checks by opening a percentage of the packages. Everything is tracked closely to ensure our customers always get the best or we can quickly remedy any issue that might sneak through the multiple QC checks. The extra time and money we save on labor and packaging supplies more than offsets this added expense and we are able to pass these saving along to our customers.

To me, designing and developing the Retail Ready Packaging is almost as complicated as developing the product itself. Thought needs to be given ahead of time as to the style of packaging to go with; sandwich style, clam shell, and gift boxes are just a few of the most commonly used. If using a hanging style for use on pegboard systems, you will need the product placement and the cutout hole to be aligned so the product hangs straight. The size of the packaging will dictate storage space, shipping and other variables. In general, you will want to minimize the packaging size while still having sufficient marketing space. Some retailers may want a short and wide design while their competitor may prefer a tall and narrow design. It is best to get feedback from anyone that you plan to have sell your product in order to help meet their needs and desires. You can always look at how similar products are packaged for ideas and best practices.

You may be tempted to use all of the available space for marketing but please resist this urge. **Less is more.** Clean and clear marketing always wins over saying everything you possibly can and potentially cluttering your tiny display area. In my opinion, we jammed too much info on the WedgeLight™ packaging, especially on the back which you will see on the next page.

Point out what the product does and what it will do for the end user. A few features and benefits can be highlighted but do not list all of them; just the main 2 or 3 should be highlighted.

Packaging may have other strategic by-products such as the obvious one of minimizing shoplifting. The packaging should protect your product and help your product sell itself. I always ask myself if the intended user picked one up off the shelf, would he or she understand the intended use and be swayed to buy the product or would they have unanswered questions?

Here is our packaging design for the Wedge Light Product:

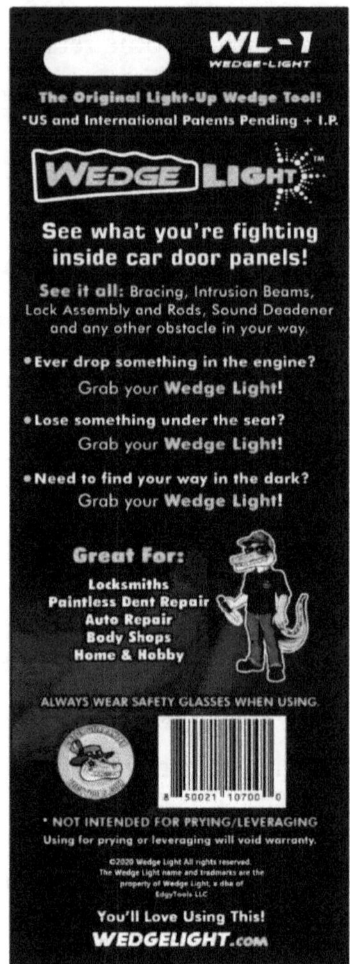

Notice the off center peg board hook opening which allows the product to hang straight. Having the Wedge positioned to the far right allows us to nest them together which saves space and protects them during transit.

You might notice the **'Push Me'** Call-To-Action at the top of the front of the Wedge Light Packaging. This is on purpose to inspire an inquisitive customer to pick up the product and try it. People are more engaged and much more likely to buy after they are holding the product in their hands. This product has a built-in shut-off timer and insane battery life, so we have no fear of over-testing or draining the battery before purchase.

You might be thinking, wow, this guy really wants to manipulate people into buying his product. I used to be 100% against selling until my paradigm was shifted. Basically, if my product or service is indeed the best, then we would be doing a disservice to the potential buyer by not selling. If a customer buys an inferior product or service because they didn't know the difference, then we would be letting them down. Please do a quick online search and watch the video "Is Selling Evil?" by Joe Polish for more info on this concept. I will discuss marketing and selling in more detail in the next chapter.

Packaging design items to consider:
Product Images
Images of the Product in Use
Dimensions
Weight
SKU#
UPC code

Features

Remember to review your notes on **Form Number 2** *in Chapter 4*

Benefits

Emotional reason to buy

Price

Website URL

Instructions or Demo URL

Warranty Information or URL

Quickstart Guide URL

Company Logo / Company Info

Trademark and/or Patent Info

QR Code

You might also need a fresh perspective because as the saying goes "You can't read the label from inside the jar". By now you are too close to your product to be unbiased. This is why I had you make good notes early on and along the way but it is a good idea to ask other's for their input as well. (By now, your product should be sufficiently protected by intellectual property (I.P.), patents, and trademarks, but still be cautious and protect yourself) As mentioned earlier, **less is more** so please do not attempt to cram all of this info into your design. **Be selective!**

PART 3 - Selling the Thing!

"If it sells itself, then you don't have to sell it."

—Stacy Streen

Marketing
Chapter 10

Marketing is the most fascinating part of the entire process to me.

Joe Polish (*I Love Marketing Podcast*) taught me the distinct difference between marketing, selling, and advertising. Many people think these three words mean the same thing but they don't. Allow me to explain it to you the way Joe taught me. Basically, **selling is what you do when you are face to face** with a potential customer or client. Note that with products, you might not get the opportunity to be face to face with many of your customers so you need to rely on packaging, websites, product listings, videos, sell sheets, and other marketing materials to do your selling for you. That was a little hint about marketing but to go a step further, **marketing is what you do to get a customer or client face to face to be sold.** Joe says a well informed (well marketed to) person will be properly positioned so that by the time they are talking to you (or on your product page) they are pre-interested, pre- motivated, pre-qualified, and pre-disposed to buy. They already want it. You do not have to sell them because they already want to buy. I consider myself an order taker, not a salesman.

The third prong is **advertising, which is basically paying to get your potential buyer to see your marketing.** Spending money to get your product (your product's marketing materials) in front of the right eyes on platforms such as search engines, social media platforms, the radio, TV commercials, etc. These are just a few examples of advertising options but there are many other ways to advertise as well. Figure out what methods work best for you, your product, and your business.

Let's say you have a website with a great video and great content to help inform your visitor and that site is converting visitors into paying customers. As long as those transactions are profitable and you can handle more of them, then you may want to pour some gas on the fire. Running ads on the most popular social media platforms and search engines might be a good next step. These would be a form of advertising which would drive traffic to your site. Of course this needs to be the right traffic, people who are interested, willing, and able to buy your product.

I am a big believer in direct marketing. This means that the marketing and advertising should be 100% trackable. It should never be a gamble. A dollar spent on marketing should return the original dollar plus the profit level you are looking to receive.

A simple example to clarify this would be if a product sells for $100 and costs you $50 total to make, package, and ship, then you have

$50 left to play with between marketing, advertising, and profit. If you spend $50 (or more) on ads to sell that product; stop, you just lost the game. However, if you can sell the product with $10 worth of ads, you just made $40 profit. Do more of that!

Figure out where your ideal customers hang out and meet them there. Each social media platform attracts a different type of person. Looking at age, in general 16-30 year olds tend to hang out in different in-person places (and on different social media platforms) than most 40-60 year olds would. Figure out which places and platforms are most relevant to your ideal customer and focus your efforts there. It is better to focus your efforts on the most appropriate platform than to spread yourself thin by trying to be on all of them.

When I market on social media platforms, I talk directly to the people in that group. I have created some of my own groups for my prospects to hang out in and I have joined tons of others as well. I do not just sell, sell, sell in the groups. I always try to provide tremendous value and insights. I make friends and thoroughly enjoy the time we share in these groups. When one of the group members mention a problem that one of my products is the best solution for, I will recommend that product along with a little tip on how to best use it for that particular situation and explain why it will work so well for them. Please note, I often recommend products made by other companies as well. Again, provide value and you will be trusted. Meet your potential customers where they already are and have some good conversations. Help them and they will trust you and people buy from people they know, like, and trust.

Marketing is like a well thought out recipe that takes a lot of ingredients to work effectively. A great recipe has been tested and tweaked for optimum results and similarly, a great marketing plan should be as well!

Some of these ingredients include, but are not limited to:

Logo

Pictures of your product

Pictures of your product in use

Video of your product in use

Video Demo including tips and best practices

Quickstart Guide

Product Page

Landing Page

Sell Sheet

Sell Sheet Video

Email Campaign: *Intro Email, 3 Reasons Email, Follow-Up Email*

Social Media Promos *in correct sizes (posts and ads)*

Webinar with introductory special

Postcards and Flyers

Grass Roots *(Word of Mouth - Tell a Friend)*

SMS / Text Messaging

Affiliate Systems

Stickers

Trade Shows

Risk Reversal – Guarantees and Warranties

Those are examples to help you get your own ideas flowing. You do not have to do any of them or you can do some or all of them.

Note: Doing just one of them really well is better than doing them all of them poorly.

Next Up: Fulfillment / Shipping

Fulfillment / Shipping
Chapter 11

Fulfillment is a big word which just means getting the product to the buyer. You are fulfilling your end of the sale. Someone purchased something from you and you need to send them what they bought or put another way, fulfill their order. This can be simply handing the customer your product if you sold it to them in person or it may involve shipping the product or even having a 3rd party fulfill it for you.

Shipping is expensive and difficult at first. There are many options as far as carriers to use. Each shipping company has their own strengths and weaknesses and I encourage you to do some research, ask questions, and get help.

I would like to briefly mention that I have even adjusted the actual size of one of my products in order to save on shipping costs. Shaving an inch off the length of this particular product allowed it to fit in a special flat rate box. The slightly smaller product worked just as well and now shipped for half the price.

You will also need shipping materials and packing supplies. Shop around and find the materials that will work best for you and your product.

You will not only want to protect your product with bubble wrap, air pockets, or some other sort of padding, but you might also want to perform the **dreaded drop test.** Basically, pack up your item like you are getting ready to ship it and then hold it out in front of your face and drop it. Can it fall to the concrete ground and remain undamaged? If the answer is no, wipe away your tears and figure out a better way to protect it or design it stronger. Trust me, I hate doing this test too but it is better to learn this yourself now versus having an upset customer informing you (and possibly the world through social media) that their product arrived broken and they want their money back and may even leave you a bad review. **Do the test.**

There are so many variables when it comes to shipping, so I will not even attempt to cover them here but do your homework. There is nothing worse than making a bunch of sales just to realize that shipping has eaten up all of your profits.

Now let's discuss storage, inventory management, and the process of reordering. **You cannot ship a product you do not have** so it is important to **know your inventory levels** and have a good system in place to track them and warn you of low levels. If your inventory is in multiple locations you will need to move product from one place to another and back which can get confusing and could lead to costly errors unless your system is easy and efficient. *(See page 59 for the form I use)*

One situation I always struggled with were trade shows. I would usually do a great job of tracking the inventory I brought to the show but after a crazy weekend including travel, lugging my product around on planes, talking with friends and customers, and pitching my products, I would be exhausted. I would come home and need to fill the orders which came in through the website while I was away. I would often not count in the inventory left over from the trade show before filling the new orders and so my inventory levels would become inaccurate. A simple form would have fixed this issue which kept repeating. Not only would my inventory have remained 100% accurate, but I would have been able to see what was stolen, lost, or given away at the show.

It sounds so simple but knowing your inventory allows you to **reorder your product in plenty of time** so you can avoid having out of stock issues. In years past, I would often not realize I needed to reorder a product until I was very low or completely out of stock. It always seemed to take the manufacturer twice as long to make my product when it was out-of-stock versus when I would reorder it before it was urgent.

It is also important to understand that the manufacturer might not be able to produce the goods in the same time-frame each time. Holidays, how busy they are, availability of supplies, shipping delays, and many other variables may cause unwanted delays so it is vital to stay ahead of the game and the only way to accomplish this is to **know your inventory numbers.**

Storage is the other item I would like to briefly touch on. When I started, I did everything out of my house. As EdgyTools® grew, I rented a storage unit close to the house and would keep my back stock inventory there. I grew to the point where I had 2 storage units and recently moved out of the two smaller units and into a very large single unit. My next step might be to rent (or purchase) a building which will allow me to reclaim my home and handle all operations out of the new location.

UPDATE: *As of the publish date, I have moved all my tools (except prototypes) out of my home and the storage unit and now a professional fulfillment center handles all of the storage and shipping for me.*

NOTE: *Make sure no matter where your products are stored, you have the **proper insurance** to protect your inventory. Speak to an insurance professional about this.*

My products are all very small, in fact I call them pocket items because most of them would literally fit in your pocket. I originally focused on designing small items because as a dent repairman myself I knew how limited the space in the work vehicle was. The strategic byproduct was saving money on both storage (warehousing) as well as shipping, which has allowed me to have the cheapest shipping fees in the industry for years.

Next Up: Making Deals

Making Deals
Chapter 12

Making one good deal can be worth the same as making hundreds or even thousands of individual sales, maybe even millions if you make a deal with a big box store! If you are marketing and selling your product yourself, you are usually selling to one customer at a time. This can be very lucrative and profitable especially since there aren't many hands in the pie. You get to keep all of the profit from each sale you make (less the cost of the manufacturing, packaging, shipping, and other costs attributed to the transaction). **"Keep it small and keep it all."**

If you make a wholesale deal, you are usually looking at selling larger quantities but at smaller profit margins since the reseller needs to make their profit as well.

There are savings of time and money with this sort of transaction as the shipping (and shipping materials) will be less than shipping the same quantity to a bunch of different addresses. You will not have to spend the same money on marketing and ads on this type of transaction. Often, the right wholesale partners will be able to move more of your product than you would be able to yourself; maybe they have been in business a long time and have a large list of people who buy from them. I encourage you to start learning about **wholesaling** as soon as possible so you can decide if you want to take this route or not.

Licensing is another type of deal you would be wise to study, even if you don't intend to license your product. You will learn how the big boys play at the highest level. These lessons will smooth your road and help you perform at a higher level.

As mentioned earlier, your end on a licensing deal may be as low as a fraction of 1% to 5% or may go up to double digit percentages. It all depends on the size of the company interested in licensing your product, what they will be doing for their part, and many other factors.

If you are licensing your product to a big box store that will handle everything, you are looking at a smaller percentage but of a huge pie. If you are licensing your product to a mid-sized company, you should be able to get a larger percentage. Keep in mind that **a good deal benefits both parties.** Do not give up too much if you aren't getting benefits in exchange but also don't negotiate such a good deal in your favor that the other party loses interest and doesn't promote your product. If the new partner isn't going to crush it, they might just list your product and sit back and wait for orders versus wanting to actively feature and promote your product.

Whichever path you choose to pursue with your product, you need to have realistic expectations and don't spend the money until it is in the bank and the dust has settled.

Always protect yourself when possible, and watch for red flags. I always recommend seeking coaching from an expert who has done this type of thing many times as well as seeking legal advice.

One line in a contract can kill everything. I have heard horror stories such as a big box store having a return clause which when reading a contract could be easily overlooked. This meant that the person had made a huge sale (tens of thousands of units) and when he drove home one day there were pallets lined up on his driveway full of his product. The big box store determined the product wasn't selling fast enough and so they sent the remainder back along with a refund demand. The big box store was completely within their rights to do this as it was written in the contract.

When I review a contract, I will spend countless hours studying each line until I fully comprehend the meaning before I even send it to my lawyer to go over with me. This allows me to ask better questions and actually understand the answers when discussing them with my lawyer. This practice also lessens the consultation time and therefore the legal bill. I also get better and better at being able to read the contacts and the legal jargon becomes more and more understandable. I am building and strengthening this skill set the more I practice and engage in it. You will improve as well.

You should start doing research on which companies you would like to do business with or have carry your product as soon as your product starts to look like a reality.

Create your "hit list" as you go so when you have your product ready, you can hit the ground running. A simple online search will get you the info you will need to start building this list. All you really need to find and list is the **Company Name, Phone Number, Email Address, and maybe a contact person's name.** What to do with this list and how to get access to the decision maker and close the deal is too involved to cover in this book. I advise you to seek the help of a coach or professional.

A lesson which I found fascinating was that there are no blank shelves in the store waiting for your product to fill them. Every inch of the store is already full of product. This means that for your product to get on the shelves, someone else's product needs to be removed. This taught me that not only did my product need to be great quality and very profitable for the store, but it had to be so much better as to justify ending what may be a long term relationship with the person or company of the product being replaced. The store might even have to discard or heavily discount the old product in order to make room for the new product. They may have invested in molds, inventory, marketing, and many other things which will also add to the cost of switching. So not only does the new product need to be a winner, it has to be such as winner as to justify changing floor plans, relationships, etc. Please think about this while you are working on developing your product. Ask yourself "What has to come out for my product to go in?".

Next Up: Financing

Financing

Chapter 13

When we are discussing financing, it is important to mention that we are all in different stages of our financial growth. Whether you are a multi-millionaire or can't buy a stick of gum, we will all face hurdles and obstacles when bringing an idea to life.

The most important factor in my opinion is selling ourselves on the idea. If you are only sort of committed then keep working your day job and your idea can become a fun story you tell about how you had that idea years ago when you see something similar in the marketplace.

However, if you are all in, passionate, and willing to do whatever it takes, then please proceed but with caution.

I love how Tony Robbins puts it that **if you don't have the resources, you just need to be more resourceful.** You can always start small and keep re-investing to become big. This is how I have always chosen to play. I look at outside financing as fuel for the fire. Early on when my operations were a mess, the last thing me or my company needed was to pour gas on the uncontrolled fires I was putting out every day.

I have learned so much about product development and selling over the last 5 years, much of which is in this book. I have put better systems and procedures in place and I have built and trained a phenomenal team. All of these things make me ready to look at outside financing as a means to go further and faster. Pouring gas on a controlled burn might make sense at this point. The irony is that once things were running so much better, I am now more profitable and no longer need outside financing.

I also would like to point out that many people (including myself) make the mistake of bringing in a partner for financial help. In my opinion, if you can qualify for a bank loan, then that is much less expensive than giving a portion of your company away. Partners should be considered if the person brings things to the table which you need and do not possess yourself. Maybe they are strong in areas you have weakness or maybe they have resources or connections that will help you. Just like with a licensing deal, partnerships can be very tricky and often do not end well. As with just about anything, **it can be very easy to get into but very difficult to get out of.** Seek advice and guidance.

NOTE: If you do not have any money to get started with, it doesn't mean you are out of the game. Many new product developers have had huge success using crowdfunding campaigns.

Next Up: Coaching and Consulting

Coaching and Consulting
Chapter 14

I am truly blessed to be in a position where people bring me their product ideas almost everyday. They ask for my advice and often offer to give me a piece of the action for my help. I love this so much because first, **it means they trust and respect me** and that means the absolute world to me! Second, **it means they are inspired and are realizing they have a bigger and brighter future ahead** of them but they need a little something. Sometimes that little something is encouragement, motivation, or advice on the next step to take. Whatever the reason, I love it!

My time and resources are limited though and if I am spending time on a call, it means I am not spending that time working on my own product ideas or businesses. **When we say "YES" to something, we are saying "NO" to something else.** That is the main reason I charge for my services. I also know and have proven that I am well worth it.

That being said, I really do love helping people so it gets confusing. To help simplify things, **I would love to hear your product idea** and if it is aligned with my interests and on the same path as my personal goals, we might work together. If it is something I can help you with but do not personally want to be invested in, this is when my coaching services might be a good fit.

I hope this book was an "easy read" for you but at the same time opened your eyes (or reminded you) about the basic fundamentals of smart product development! I wish you happiness and success. I am rooting for you to win!

Please share your successes and wins (big or small) with me on social media so we can celebrate together!

To help make sure that I see it, please use the following hashtags:

#inventing, #inventingbook, #davestreen

I look forward to seeing your product on the shelves!

To request help or to chat about product development, please visit:

Talk2Dave.com

P.S. If you hear someone say "I've got a million dollar idea", please let them know about this book. You'll be their hero, and mine!

Notes

____

____

____

____

____

____

____

____

____

____

____

____

____

____

Special Thanks

I credit much of my success to my wife, Stacy, of over 25 years. She has always encouraged and supported me to chase my dreams. Thanks to my Mom and Dad for invoking my entrepreneurial spirit. Also, thank you to my Uncle Richard, and my Nanno (Italian for Grandpa) who was written up as the best foundry man in the US; they both taught me how things work, how to identify problems, and how to fix them.

Thank you to Joe Polish for teaching me marketing and Dan Sullivan for giving me even more courage and confidence in business. Special thanks goes to Marino (Atari Joystick Patent Holder) who taught me so much about engineering, manufacturing, and the whole process. I'd also like to thank Jim, Marino's incredible CAD guy, for his contributions over the years. Big thanks to Michael Miller for sharing his vast product development wisdom with me.

Finally, I would like to thank Archie, Lori, Robert, and the rest of the WeHelpAuthors team for their help with this book, our websites, and marketing efforts. Your contributions have made all of the difference!

Chad Johnson, Timothy Paulson, and Paul Graziosi – I'm forever grateful! To the countless other people who have taught me and influenced me in my life. – Thank you!

Note from the author to you, the reader:

This is the exact playbook I developed for my own companies out of necessity. It took me from the brink of bankruptcy to earning a very comfortable living! It helped simplify the process and keep everything in one place and on track. I absolutely love helping people make their dreams a reality and I am pretty darn successful at it so please do not hesitate to reach out for my coaching and consulting services.

Your friend in Product Development,

Dave

Someone like you wrote this book.
We helped.

If you've considered writing your own,
do not try to figure it out alone.

WeHelpAuthors takes you from idea to published author.